The Coldest Places

Heather Hammonds

Contents

Cold Weather   2

The Coldest Place   4

Ice on the Sea   6

Cold Islands   8

Big Mountains   10

Rivers of Ice   12

People in the Coldest Places   14

Glossary   16

Cold Weather

In winter,
it can get very cold.
On cold days,
we put on warm clothes.
We stay inside
and keep warm.

In some places,
it is very cold all the time.

The Coldest Place

This is the Antarctic. It is the coldest place on Earth.

In winter, it is very dark and windy.

4

Some animals live here.
They live on land
and in the sea.
Penguins get their food
from the sea.

Ice on the Sea

This cold place is the Arctic.
There is ice on the sea
in winter and in summer.
Look at the big **icebergs**!

This big bear can live
on the ice.
It swims in the cold sea.

Cold Islands

It is very cold and windy
on this **island**.
Some plants grow here,
but there are no trees.

Seals live on this cold island.
They sit on the rocks
and swim in the sea.

Big Mountains

It is very cold
at the top of big **mountains**.
There is snow and ice
on the mountains.

Big animals called yaks
live by the mountains.
They have thick fur
to keep them warm.

Rivers of Ice

There are rivers of ice
in this cold place.
The ice goes down
into the sea.

Animals live in the water
and on the land
by the rivers of ice.

People in the Coldest Places

People can live and work in very cold places.

Some people live
by big mountains, too.
They keep warm
inside their houses.

Glossary

icebergs

island

mountains